Poetic Pespectives

JERREL E. WOLFE

BOOKSIDE Press

Copyright © 2022 by Jerrel E. Wolfe

ISBN: 978-1-990695-74-2 (Paperback)

978-1-990695-75-9 (E-book)

All rights reserved. No part of this publication may be reproduced, distributed, or transmitted in any form or by any means, including photocopying, recording, or other electronic or mechanical methods, without the prior written permission of the publisher, except in the case brief quotations embodied in critical reviews and other noncommercial uses permitted by copyright law.

The views expressed in this book are solely those of the author and do not necessarily reflect the views of the publisher, and the publisher hereby disclaims any responsibility for them. Some names and identifying details in this book have been changed to protect the privacy of individuals.

BookSide Press
877-741-8091
www.booksidepress.com
orders@booksidepress.com

CONTENTS

Dedication
Reaching For The Stars..9
Poets Legacy...11
"Excitement of Life"...12
Forever..14
Geisha...16
Men watch your lady slumber 18
Riding for your friend 20
My Pap..23
This Place...24
Today I Met An Angel...25
A Legend Remembered...29
With You...30
Poetic Angel...32
Tools Of Life...34
Embryo...36
Escape 38
Perhaps 41
Entranced..43
Purpose 45
Childhood..47
My Kitchen Window...50
Inspiration 52
Johnny Cash...53
The Photo...55

The Archeologist	57
A Ivory Tribute	59
Heather	60
Nature	62
Free Spirit	64
Becoming You	66
Kisses at the top, Laughter at the bottom	68
Birthdays	71
The Graduate	72
Adopted	74
Still Healing - Still Feeling	77
Damn Damn Double Damn	79
Poetic Bastardization	81
I Know	82
History In The Distance	84
I Led The Black To Battle	86
Death March	88
Today's War	90
Owed Respect	92
Respected Sacrifice	94
An Honored Gift	95
To your honor	98
At Rest	99
Candy	103
Trick or Treat	105
Ghosts ships of Nantucket	107
The Haunted Saxophone	109
Easter Wish	110
Heavens Valentine	111
A Christmas Book	113
Let Us Win	116
Abandoned	119
Chicago	123

Selma	126
Origami	128
In God We Trust	130
The Postal Carrier	132
I Found It In Miami	134
I Am The Seasons - You Are the Wind	136
Taken	138
Father Time	139
Recipe for Life	142
The Fishin Hole	145
The Zoo Keeper	148
Summoning of the White Horse	150
Soulmate	153
Summers Gone	155
A Place In Time	156
Each Day	158
Growing, Growing, ...Gone	159
Chess Master/Chess Charmer	161
Breeching Death	165
Independence Day	167
New Beginnings	169
Twilight Years	171

Dedication

I am blessed to have received a gift to pass on throughout time. The words, wisdom, discernment, and ponderings penned to parchment, in the pages of Poetic Perspectives, are dedicated to my grandchildren Sullivan Malone, and Delaney Baker, as well as all future grandchildren.

Reaching For The Stars

This poet is quite humbled
by words spoken here
How many lives that have been touched
how many stopped to hear

The rhyme and the meter
both have come to life
In the mastery of the pieces
I write for you tonight

It's you my faithful followers
who look into this site
Inspire me with your comments
such uplifting words you write

With you as my backbone
I venture forth from here
Publish and produce a book
it's all not very clear

You say I have the talent
my words have recieved much praise
Labeled masterpieces by your pens
my hopes and skills you've raised

Jerrel E. Wolfe

Now as I write this book
I need you all you see
You are my inspiration
my steadfast tall oak tree

I've been said to be the new blood
a storied poet of such rhyme
My name will stand with noted poets
till the end of time

I'm trusting in your wisdom
it's what's inspired me
To leap into the future
this realm of poetry

Poetic Perspectives

Poets Legacy

I picture not a pastel hue
on pages where words
create a crowded view

But seeing past what's written here
the colored parchment
has no fear

Ready for what may befall...
the artists pen
out shines them all

With words that mesmerize and hold
One's feelings trapped
in poetic mold

For it's here inscribed for all to see
the love, the joy, the artistry
The lasting beauty just might be

This Poets Final Legacy

Jerrel E. Wolfe

"Excitement of Life"

There's birth and death and in between
and that is all we have
A time spent within this space
it's called LIFE...for us to grab

We must endure the dangers
to reap the happiness that safety brings
This is called "The Excitement of Life"
love and the pleasure of things

With daily stress the excitement fades
and the resulting lifestyle pleasures
Our brains emit the chemicals
in unregulated measures

Without the pleasure
comes the anger distress and so much pain
The "Excitement of Life" has left us
and we long for it's regain

We try to find it in a job
a club or just with friends
A look outside the marriage
is where this message ends

For you see "The Excitement of Life"
is born down deep inside
It's brought to the surface
with honor work and pride

Believing in the Man above
and His direction you follow
Will grant you peace and harmony
everywhere you go

Yes we all need that "Excitement"
to fill our hearts with cheer
Be careful where you look for it
God's test is not often clear

Jerrel E. Wolfe

Forever

There was something in the air that night
that our eyes first did meet
The feeling that came over me
consumed me from head to feet

The voice soft and pleasant
the touch so warm and sweet
The time we spent together
sparked passionate romantic heat

Seems not long ago
that candle burned deep inside of me
It's flame forever brightened
by the fuel of harmony

Two candles burn as one
in this life of yours and mine
A love so true and tender
it stands the test of time

And with fifty years behind us
I just thought that you should know...
My candle burns as bright tonight
as it did so long ago

So darling if I'm called one night
without a chance to tell you so
Look nightly unto the heavens
and search out my candle's glow

Jerrel E. Wolfe

Geisha

The cherry blossoms and the bonsai tree
create an image throughout time
Of a Geisha's beauty etched in the walls
and placed in a dark corner of my mind

At ninety in this rocking chair
I pull forth an angel's face
Dressed in her kimona
entering a room with so much grace

There was point in life I knew
that life's emotional jar was filled
For I had been through a real world war
to view children and brothers killed

From horror to perfection
in such a short amount of time
I stuffed her in the closet
just to endure this life of mine

Short circuit...call it overload
the mind couldn't take all that
The door was shut I left her
just about 60 long years back

And today as I dig into
that corner of my mind
The horror's all subsided
it's just the beauty I can find

The beauty of the ladies
whom God has placed upon this land
To help us endure this life
and upon us place their hand

Another day sitting in this chair
looking past the ocean bluff
I find no beauty that has 'er surpassed
God's creation meant for us

If I leave this world with one parting thought
for all men to confide
It would be to find the love of a lady
to fulfill your earthly ride

Jerrel E. Wolfe

Men watch your lady slumber

She lays there slumbering through the night
her daily chores been done
Executive things the hectic stuff
and lots of errands run

She's tucked in boy wonder
fed the dog and changed the bed
Checked on the homework
ironed some then just read

This day was quite the normal
for you just must see
This is a mom's life so much strife
and tears we never see

She will love me in the morning
have a smile upon her face
Send the children off to school
with another loving embrace

Then tidy up
check the time and hurry to her place
Where she will work a burdensome job
in todays rat race

There's not much time for others
lifes filled with too much dear
Herself has placed upon a shelf
her needs her wants and fear

So when you see a lady slumbering
either night or day
Place a prayer upon her
and look to God and say...

I know you've placed upon woman
a really heavy task
Protect her sooth and help her
this is really all I ask

Yes you have your reasons
women work this way
I know there's a lot of clean up
at the end of every day

Your power is so magnificent
you can create a soul like this
To toll through life be a wife
and live in peaceful bliss

Jerrel E. Wolfe

Riding for your friend

My thoughts were clouded as I went to bed last night
so I summoned forth my steed of white
To carry me in dreams from here
and place me at your side

I know not why this bothered me
but I knew in you I had to see
the reason for this ride

Seventeen hands high
...this steed could fly
His wings unfurled
towards heaven's sky

Now firmly in the saddle
of this white horse I've come to know
I see the future I see the past
and places I can go

Emanating from my soul
a horse comes forth this way
For me to call upon
on any given day

Tonight I ride to touch the heart
of one so near and dear
A special gifted lady
whom I can see through quite clear

This trip not really needed
no emergency in sight
My steed thinks I must be at her side
on this starlit night

And now as we glide from the heavens
I see her in the park
A true and trusted friend
walks with her in the dark

I listen quite intently
as we walk behind them so
Then place a gentle nudge upon them
to direct them where to go

She felt it as she look up
wondering what this sign might be
It was me upon that tall white horse
a vision she could not see

Jerrel E. Wolfe

My friend still walks with her
through her life of pain sorrow
Giving hope and caring
both for today and tomorrow

I see no other purpose
for us to be here this summers night
So I summon my companion
...my special steed of white

We too have reached into the heart
of one who is quite troubled
The number of her needed friends
has just little more than doubled

And if she calls upon us
on nights of pain and anguish
We'll glide right there...touch her hair
...wink nod and vanish

My Pap

Shoes sit silent on the floor
the coat hangs on the tree
The scent of the man still lingers
he's left not here for me

At six he was my idle
at ten sat by his side
Now I sit here
fond memories and tears I hide

Pap you've walked many a mile
if those shoes could only talk
The prints they've made won't fade away
like shadows down the block

For when I turn life's corners
I'll walk the path you've laid
Reflecting upon your footsteps
with the family you have made

Jerrel E. Wolfe

This Place

Cool breeze blows this Saturday morn
as the Mississippi flows
I sit here on this riverside bench
not knowing where life goes

I'm blessed with health and memories abound
of family friends and this wonderful town
The jazz the laughs the street car sounds
good food the history of this seaport town

Birds seek the crumbs
ants walk the cracks
I see I'm as small as they
For in 30 years the river flows and I'll have gone away

And yet God's brought me to this bench
to watch the river flow
Now to honor the request
of a homeless man I don't even know

In this gift I see my purpose
God walks with me today
Spirits now lifted
I'm off to enjoy the day

Today I Met An Angel

Today I viewed a headstone
worn and tilted over time
I saw a name upon it
very similar to mine

I know there was no relationship
I... but a thousand miles away
The inscription there upon it
said miss Jesse... born a slave

In my mind I traveled back in time
I felt the autumns breeze
I fell into a dreamlike state
as I sat amongst the leaves

And I as a caring soul
walked in the past as if a ghost
Into a room with Jesse Morgan
with the ones she loved the most

-

Jerrel E. Wolfe

Tired and drained and full of pain
she made it to her chair
Slowly turning to align just right
she eased her bottom there

A sigh blew past her parted lips
as her shoulders dropped in place
The wear and tear of many years
was etched upon her face

A sweetness still exuded
from her fraile southern voice
As she spoke about her children
in a life that had no choice

Miss Jesse kept the mansion
in its elegant southern grace
Tended to the inside
master's children not her race

Thirteen children she had bore
in her eighty three years in this place
Her wrinkles told a story
as I stared upon her face

Poetic Perspectives

Taken from her loving touch
sold on any day
Some barely able to walk or talk
just simply swept away

Now in the dimness
of the Autumn's pale sunlight
She speaks into the shadows
to her chillun with delight

Theres Thomas he's the tall one
with scars upon his back
George Earl and Sarah
all the little ones around they sat

They looked upon their dying mother
as she gently passed away
Saying to all...I love you
In the last breath took that day

–

Jerrel E. Wolfe

Now
The leaves blow round the headstone
as if children drawing near
To hug their loving mother
and keep her warm this time of year

We'll never really know the love
of a family torn this way
Lest we pause and look into the past
in the dim light of a harvest day

Poetic Perspectives

A Legend Remembered

A love for his wife
A love for his child
A love for all nature
A love for the wild

Of all words available
To describe this honorable Christian man
LOVE... was the last grain
To fall from the hourglass of his hand

Jerrel E. Wolfe

With You

Come to me this winter's eve
and place your head upon my chest
Immerse yourself in my loving touch
find peace and happiness

Think not of the day gone by
or of the one to come
Breathe in my scented fragrance
together with the soul you've won

Then take this soul inside you
and bathe it in your heart
Melt my love into your being
and drift away in thought

Fix your eyes upon the moon
the stars and dark of night
Feel nothing but my essence
and know this love is right

Should you chance to see a shooting star
blaze across your late night sky
Imagine us upon it
if the two of us could fly

Going to another place
where two hearts beat as one
Cuddling in a feather bed
where silken sheets were spun

There we spend eternity
immersed in perfect bliss
Finding all that's needed
in your loving kiss

Jerrel E. Wolfe

Poetic Angel

In a world of many cultures
languages and such
There is no such power
as the human touch

It can give hope and enlighten
even bring a smile
Show the love sent from above
and cover many miles

I am a worldly traveler
...an angel...maybe so
I find all this pleasure
in every place I go

I've touched the hands of Kenyans
the sick and homeless there
Traveled to the Philippines
to place hands upon their hair

It's a small thing that I have to give
my smile and tender touch
The joy that it brings back
is cherished oh so much

So if your ever needy
or need a place to pray
Or just some simple caring
to get you through the day

Know that I am with you
my touch you might not feel
You'll gain some strength from my drink
of deep love and good will

Jerrel E. Wolfe

Tools Of Life

Walking on these two feet
that God has given me
I travel to the places
Earth's great beauty I do see

With these hands I reach out to touch
what my eyes can only see
With this heart I feel the love
that's placed inside of me

With ears I hear the echo's
of trains passing in the night
Hear the sounds of nature
its marvelous delight

Gifts are bestowed upon us
from the Creator up above
Produced in His image
with the main ingredient ...Love

It's time to pause and think today
of where we all have been
What has touched upon our senses
that we've let enter in

Poetic Perspectives

Each one of us needs to give thanks
for the life we've come to know
Cherish all the moments
that's set our hearts aglow

Jerrel E. Wolfe

Embryo

What's this that causes me to stir
and test the boundaries here
A newness fills this habitat
a sense that's not to clear

Yesterday was nothing
but today a warmth is here
A melody is playing
there's singing in my ear

I feel a rhythmic motion
and reach to press this mass
Of whats become my kingdom
so many questions I must ask

Angels speak to me
in this womb of what's called mother
Who will take me on a journey
and love me like no other

What is this love I'm told of
and excitement of which they speak
Why are my angelic images
just a blur and out of reach

Poetic Perspectives

What is purpose
and who is God
What is light
and a path to trod

They say
I will have no fear
That my time
is very near

To accept the gifts
that come my way
Live what's called life
from day to day

I will be called child
baby and more
When my guardian angel
leads me through the door

Jerrel E. Wolfe

Escape

I've never had a Christmas
with the love of family
They said I was sent to a home
before the age of three

And there I spent my youthful life
till old enough to leave
Till finally... I up and ran
one starry Christmas eve

At the local rail yard
I reached out for the train
A hand reached out and grabbed me
from a faced wretched in pain

"Hello, I'm Bo Baggins"
he spoke into the night
As he fell back into the railcar
in the dark and out of sight

I told him my name's Billie
and from where I had come
I told him of my story
and why I had to run

He told me this was his final ride
after years of riding rails
That after 70 years of this
his aging health had failed

I heard stories of the great depression
and homeless families
Tragedies and heartaches
and cast out refugees

He said he had a gift for me
to bestow at the light of day
Something to carry with me
as I traveled along my way

And so we sat and talked a bit
in the dim light of a waning moon
Then we drifted off to sleep
it would be daylight very soon

The morning sun broke through the door
my crusted eyes did part
To finally see Bo Baggins
motionless in the shadows of past dark

Jerrel E. Wolfe

Merry Christmas I spoke out from the heart
to a man who befriended me
It didn't take long to realize
the lack of response that came from he

As the railcar rocked from side to side
and the wheels clanged on the rail
I realized Bo had moved on from this life
in search of his holy grail

There in his outstretched hand
was the gift he offered me
A shiny golden pocket watch
with an inscription that did read...

Eternal Life Awaits Thee

Perhaps

Today I saw a headstone
with earth piled by its side
A year of life etched in granite
A tiny child had died

Just what was his purpose
what effect did he have here
It seems it was a waste of life
God's reasoning's so unclear

Perhaps he brought back together
the love of a man and wife
Perhaps he changed the time line
and saved a nurse's life

Perhaps he provided a year of joy
to a soul wretched in pain
Perhaps he inspired a poet
to pick up his pen again

Perhaps his bright eyes made God smile
perhaps God needed one pure soul…
To carry on a task in heaven
or just to have his story told

Jerrel E. Wolfe

It's a question with no answer
Perplexing as it might be
I stand here firm in my convictions
knowing that I believe

Poetic Perspectives

Entranced

In the darkness of a summer's night
I lay upon the bed
While staring at the ceiling
my thoughts are being read

In silence I reach into the deep
and flow my thoughts to Him
Shadows gently moving
outdoor lights are shining in

My mind and soul have become one
all energy is displaced
There is a direct connection
with His amazing grace

With humbleness I question
if my deeds are just and right
That I am moving forward
reaching for the light

I seek the youth ahead of me
not the youth of the past
While passing on the wisdom
that life placed in my grasp

Jerrel E. Wolfe

Released...I inhale the power
soul now back in its place
Movement and expression
has returned unto my face

A cooling breeze flows 'oer my skin
my mind breaks free from Him
Feeling all is right this night
I smile and dream again

Purpose

Today the sun stretched up to God
the birds chirped in the trees
I found myself lying in the grass
watching busy honey bees

Cool breezes crossed my furrowed brow
as I pondered life this day
Seeing worth in each of us
which some just throw away

A mind a talent a purpose for which
life's meaning shows its light
Yet we live in such a harried world
purpose seems quite trite

So many live without it
not seeing why they're here
Struggling with life from day to day
moving from year to year

Heed the message in this piece
pause to stop and think
It's not about the me or I
It's what's written in this ink

Jerrel E. Wolfe

For you there is a reason
a purpose for your being
A need to commune with your God
connect with what He's seeing

There in lies your answers
to all lifes up's and down's
With purpose laid before you
bright eyes erase your frown's

Poetic Perspectives

Childhood

To live each day of childhood
is such a simple joy
Playing from the time you wake
or opening a brand new toy

As children we may want for not
as parents guide us right
Good parents cover our wants and needs
and tuck us in each night

Instilled with direction and manners
we children continually grow
Gaining trust and stature
and knowledge we've come to know

When reaching adolescence
we seek to become young adults
Many choices are laid upon us
we show our many faults

With each daily conquest
to reach up to that place
We leave a little childhood
behind us in that space

Jerrel E. Wolfe

We choose to drive an auto
seek an opposite to kiss
Test the childhood boundaries
and leave a life of bliss

I challenge all young children
who read this poetic rhyme
Cherish all your childhood
while you have the time

For once you've crossed the boundary
of alcohol and sex
Your childhood is forever lost
you've taken the adult test

You can never go back
be what you used to be
You've become accountable
to accept the consequence you see

You just might have a baby
wreck the family car
Be drunk and kill your best friend
become forever scarred

Poetic Perspectives

Are you really up for this
it's time to stop and think
Adulthood is forever
don't let heartache break that link

When you've come to realize
the message deep in this
Love and respect your parents
who instilled their loving kiss

You'll cross that line with wisdom
and the power to achieve
You'll forever live with childhood in your heart
until this earth that you do leave

Jerrel E. Wolfe

My Kitchen Window

Of all the places in my nest
that I would like to be
I find peace in my kitchen
and the window from which to see

The children have all come and gone
my husband's passed his test
Today I'll tidy up a bit
and view that robin's nest

Last Christmas there was snowflakes
a blanket of virgin snow
Tree branches kissed with heavens touch
lit by a winter moons softened glow

I've watched squirrels hoard their acorns
playing in the autumn leaves
Viewed the picturesque folage
and the aging of the trees

There's been roses in my garden
tulips beneath the pine
From this kitchen window
I've enjoyed this life of mine

Today I'll pass this window on
to the new owner of my home
Tell her of the joy it's been
in the life that I have known

It's just a kitchen window
with a view for one to see
The joys of God's creation
that He made for you and me

Inspiration

Learning to live learning to love
learning the values instilled from above
Building a family building a life
building a legacy with children and wife

Today I live at the right hand of God
building another home
Preparing for my family
with the seeds that I have sewn

My journey sometimes arduous
My life a work of art
I've planted seeds of love and faith
and I leave one loving thought

It's only love that sets us free
from this world and all its strife
It's God's grace and mercy
that through His child I have new life

Johnny Cash

The scent upon that pillow
today still lingers there
The laughter that was upon it
no longer fills the air

God chose to take a man away
who walked a narrow path
Enjoyed the trees the animals
and always made you laugh

He could always find the humor
in a world possessed with fear
This man could quote the scripture
and make you turn an ear

His life was filled with purpose
singing songs of joy and praise
This stately man dressed in black
could make your eye brows raise

The uniqueness of his southern voice
grabbed you in the heart
No other man before him could match
the talent of his art

Jerrel E. Wolfe

Yes Johnny Cash we'll miss you
your notes won't fill my ear
Each time I hear your golden hits
I'll know your spirits near

The Photo

Another year has come and gone
for my existence in this place
Time has moved by oh so fast
it barely shows upon my face

Perhaps another wrinkle
or some whitening of the hair
Such a subtle change in me
with this photo I compare

But to my left my mother
and to the right my dad
Both have vanished from my life
It leaves me very sad

'Or the decades I have seen them
once or twice a year
My life is very busy
entrenched in my career

With pride they sent me on my way
when I was twenty one
Successful in the corporate world
many victories I had won

Jerrel E. Wolfe

Today I look back on this life
with photo in my hand
Wishing I had spent time with them
while they walked upon this land

I never really got to know them
the two who gave me life
Too busy in this corporate world
for children or a wife

I never asked about their love
or even how they met
My youthful time was to often spent
taking what I could get

And now what's left's a picture
of a family I once had
For God has called to heaven
the two called Mom and Dad

The Archeologist

Tired and drained from digging
in the hot Italian sun
I drifted into a dream like state
to where this story had begun

Klopping hoof steps echoed through the streets
fog rolled in from the coastal bay
Bells tolled in the distance
in the city of Pompei

The Roman ships lay anchored
the harbour reflected dim light
The smell of ashe was in the air
Vesuvius grumbled this summer's night

The rumble was no different
than that of nights before
Citizens went about their lives
and did their evening chores

The crash of a mighty explosion
brought the city to its feet
It was over in just minutes
this metropolis met defeat

Jerrel E. Wolfe

Hurled from the massive mountain
plumes of earth and ashe
Firey rocks from Hell had come
to reap destruction for the mass

Startled I awaken
to see what today remains of this
The framework of a city
recovered from this abiss

I feel this horrid nightmare
as I walk the ancient street
View into the distance
its Vesuvius my eyes meet

Its power and its beauty
are quite overwhelming to me
As I reach back for my shovel
to uncover history

Poetic Perspectives

A Ivory Tribute

Today I touched the ivory
of a keyboard from the past
Sat upon that piano bench
and looked deep into my glass

Yes it makes great music
but why did death bestow
God's creature that walked this earth
that we've come to cherish so

I'll never understand the need
to kill just for the sport
To poach endangered species
wealthy hunters and thugs consort

We've all been granted a life to live
in a world so very fine
Its beauty overwhelming
its creatures so divine

Today I pray it's different
this is not supposed to be
In honor of those slain for fame
I'll play a symphony

Jerrel E. Wolfe

Heather

Captured in that photo
a picture on the page
The beauty of a loved one
never more to age

A smile warm as any sunset
full of radiant glow
Entranced in the moment
her thoughts we'll never know

This timeless treasure
sits atop the desk
for all my world to see
Now I await the moment
that her love comes back to me

Picked up on a stormy night
on the far side of the town
It was all so unexpected
that her new car would break down

Now forty days have passed
since I've heard that lovely voice
Praying each and every day
our lives will again rejoice

Poetic Perspectives

Again life yields no answers
to why this all must be
Why my faith is being tested
as I drown in this Earthly bleed

So I pray and view this picture
sitting atop the desk
Holding to my faith in God
as I wrestle with this test

Jerrel E. Wolfe

Nature

The harvest moon shines bright tonight
through branches bare of leaves
Reflecting off the placid lake
into the forest filled with trees

Each trunk stands as a sentinel
guarding all within
The darkened shadows hide the life
peering out again

The crickets and the bullfrogs
perform their dutys' here each night
Unveiling a wall of protective utterings
keeping safe those out of sight

Step not into the shadows
or from the boat in which you sit
For eyes are intently on you
and nature's radar never quits

The forest in the night time
is not meant for you and me
It's meant for all God's creatures
who search for harmony

Poetic Perspectives

Tomorrow is another day
where life roams the Earth again
Foraging for another meal
to survive those known as men

When the sun has fallen
beneath the sentinels beyond this lake
Mother nature will take back over
and a sensus she will take

She'll cull with fire and pestilence
the creatures there within
Satisfied with her duty
a new day will begin

Jerrel E. Wolfe

Free Spirit

I thought I heard a whisper
beneath the tall pine trees
Faint sounds of a long lost lover
brought me to my knees

There upon the forest floor
I sat in disbelief...
To see a distant vision
of the one that caused me grief

Life had come full circle
for a man who believed in God
New love and growing friendships
and a promising path to trod

For now she is still out there
this ghost etched in my mind
Wondering through the massive pines
with no body in which to find

How long will she be there
and where will her path lead
Could there be a body living
without a soul to feed

Poetic Perspectives

Free Spirit...that's the answer
for one who walks this way
Empty shells never get to heaven
and lost souls walk day to day

Jerrel E. Wolfe

Becoming You

Credits rolled on a blackened screen
people's printed name
Who found themselves in a troubled world
and laid their claim to fame

We all have that hidden talent
to aspire to grow and be
Happy with the career we choose
and work in peaceful serenity

Just how do we find it
search the depths inside
To do what makes us happy
and fill life's work with pride

We have so many talents
choices we can make
But when looked at life through God's eyes
there is but one path to take

Some of us do find it
and live life with a smile
Looking forward to the tomorrows
in a career that's so worthwhile

Poetic Perspectives

The secret I find to finding this
career of happy bliss
Is just asking for direction
for the lives you want to kiss

Hold faith and seek direction
looking toward your goal
With rewards placed upon you
your pathway will unfold

Kisses at the Top, Laughter at the Bottom

Did you ever take a coaster ride
500 feet off the ground
One there just to travel straight
with no ups and downs

If you had a chance to live your life
on a scale of 1-10
Would you choose to live it
from 1-5, or 6-10

For 1-5's depression
to the happiness you have
6-10's the love you share
and laughter from inside

Our lives have become too hectic
to seek to laugh and play
When we seem to have the time
the laughter's gone away

Poetic Perspectives

We can find the time to be serious
and maybe let out a chuckle
In the reality of all this
under stress we seem to buckle

So we live life on a scale of 1-5
as so many years go by
Not realizing what is a 10
with laughter in the sky

When riding this rollercoaster
and I need to bring it down
I lay some tender kisses
upon her furrowed crown

If I choose that level 6
as the place I want to be
I need to move those kisses
to the lips saved just for me

Jerrel E. Wolfe

For us our life's a rollercoaster
that rides from 6-10
It starts with love and ends with laughter
and all that enters in

It's kisses at the top
laughter at the bottom
We ride the speeding bullet
no tickets...we don't need 'em

I love this rollercoaster ride of life
and being free to ride it
To laugh each day along the way
and have KISS control to guide it

Birthdays

Birthdays come and birthdays go
can you remember all of the past
All the cards and blessings
the gifts and toys amassed

Can you think back just a decade
or for some maybe two
Remember all the joy you had
and those that were there for you

Can you see what was important
can you feel the real intent
Of those who took the time to care
and all the love they sent

This birthday are you sorry
for the selfishness as you grew
Not realizing the real message sent
from all the lives you knew

With age comes perspective
wisdom and consciousness
Gifts of smiles and blessings
provide your happiness

Jerrel E. Wolfe

The Graduate

Today I hold the parchment
that I had worked for all my life
Now looking forward
I see a job three children and a wife

I'm standing at the threshold
of a life I'm sure to find
To live this American dream
that plays out in my mind

I'm blessed to have great parents
a girlfriend that is true
The knowledge and the wisdom
and the courage to play through

But before I seek my future
there's l price that I must pay
Follow my father's footsteps
and serve my country right away

You see there are many factions
that would take this all from me
Care nothing of my future
and my love for family

Poetic Perspectives

Tomorrow I'll become a Marine
and I'll help defend this land
Do it all for God and country
and the honored men who made their stand

I may be called to go to war
I just might lose my life
But if I am blessed to come through this test
I will have three children and a wife

Jerrel E. Wolfe

Adopted

At sixteen I had lived a life
of fun filled memories
A mother and a father
with two sisters there to please

But from a distant cousin
words fell upon my ear...
"You see you've been adopted
and you're not really dear."

My parents sat in hesitation
as I pinned them to the wall
Asked them why they held it back
knowing they knew it all

The response was but " we love you
you need not know the past
All that is important is that
our love will forever last."

"NO mother... you don't get it
there's something missing in my life
Now that it's discovered
I live each day in strife."

Poetic Perspectives

With pills I tried to ease the pain
of why I was left abandoned
Wrapped up in a blanket
my future to daycare handed

She never ever came back
perhaps tried when I was seven
Now with forty three years past
I wonder if she's in heaven

I've lived my life in wonderment
I wonder if so has she
Even though I'm settled
there's something missing here from me

~~~~~~

A thought I pass on to all parents
who choose to adopt another
Tell them early of the past they have
and love them like no other

Jerrel E. Wolfe

You'll be accepted as a mom and dad
and loved because you're caring
Not lay upon your child
The pain so overbearing

Still Healing - Still Feeling

Today I sit in a place
I dare not want to be
Thinking of the one I love
so far away from me

The caring soul that saved me
from a catastrophic mess
Now finds her love enslaved to me
challenged by this test

There is no other woman
whom I love and hold so dear
Emotions seem to wain a bit
I hurt and still have fear

I'm told it really takes a while
to get over a love now passed
Even when it seems like this
is just inches from my grasp

This wretched soul keeps climbing
the walls to be set free
Somehow never getting there
past love is holding me

Jerrel E. Wolfe

With rational and reason
I know I must move on
To find my destined future
and sing a different song

My new love oh so wonderful
is stagnant in the mist
Waiting for my heart to release
the anger of past bliss

To look into the future
is very hard for me
So this person in my past
is purged with poetry

The Lord My God has given me
this talent to possess
Soon my heart and soul shall sail
to a new found happiness

I can't control the currents
or help the wind to blow
I must be patient in the fact
the futures His you know

Poetic Perspectives

Damn Damn Double Damn

Twas a gift I had been waiting for
for nearly a whole year
Saved up all my money
and paid a price so dear

Arriving in a pure white box
it weighed twenty pounds or so
I couldn't wait to get inside
to build it don't you know

Undressed and laid out in a row
the pieces made a mess
Instructions packaged in the box
made this a simple test

To open them was such a chore
the plastic taped up to the max
I couldn't wait to open them
I just wanted all the facts

First Spanish then German
Japanese and French
Where the hell is English...
Oh...the back page it presents

Jerrel E. Wolfe

"A" goes here and "B" goes there
I can't find bolts "X" and "Y"
Who in the heck packaged this...
some annoying dweeb of a guy

Refer to page three column two
for the template and the drilling
I found my chargeable drill
but the battery is not willing

Okay lets just skip that part
now feeling half a man
If I can just find the base
I'll do the best I can

Who needs these damn instructions
the next paragraph is French
I finally know just what I need...
a metric crescent wrench

Poetic Bastardization

It is with hesitation and trepidation
that I find myself in this situation
I need eradication and an activation
for the generation of good jubilation

With that an earned vacation
to the shores of this great nation
A summerization for the culmination
of this poetic creation

With no humiliation frustration or damnation
It did not take much concentration
To bait with this crustation
the rusty hook cast out for duration

Now a sun tan for healthy beautification
a fish will be the finalization
One great meal for my edification
I hope will not yield to a vaccination

Jerrel E. Wolfe

I Know

Your feelings are worn upon your sleeve
I know you know I know
My heart is mending by your touch
I know you know I know

I know you as a true friend
a companion sent for me
I know you know I love you
it's very hard for me

You know I know the love of fifty
is not the same as twenty three
I know you know the challenges
facing you and me

You know I seek your voice at night
I know you seek mine too
I know that there's great passion
in two lives that were so blue

You know I know you very well
I know you know the fear
We are both rebounding
the futures not so clear

I know you know I'll travel
across the many miles
To work on this relationship
and bring you more than smiles

I know I know you know
I know you know I know
The bond grows deep between us
in a love we've come to know

Jerrel E. Wolfe

History In The Distance

The narrow streets and cobblestone paths
speak history to me
Visions of the British
their pillage from the sea

They came at night and raided
those who sought a distant refuge
The lives that could not be left alone
their souls continually abused

Militia was the early name
known as minute men by a few
Upon them lay the mighty task
That could end a life that they once knew

They scrambled in the darkness
screams of children and great fear
Would they make it back tonight
or would a bullet pierce them dear

The ladies gathered in support
the men were brave and true
When the final musket rung
they knew the battle's through

Poetic Perspectives

In silence soulmates gathered
and viewed down narrow streets
Listened to the cobblestones
to hear their loved ones feet

When in the distant shadows
they caught a moving glimpse
Twas the weary men of battle
frightened hearts became less intense

Cheers rose from the porches
the ring of churches' bell
Greeted the returning minute men
from the gates of hell

It's just another story
one that the pavement speaks to me
When I look down that narrow street
that leads to history

Jerrel E. Wolfe

I Led The Black To Battle

Men this is the last time
I will speak to the 54th today
The charge that is upon us
will no doubt end in disarray

When the cannons rumble
that's when we'll make our stand
Over the wall and down that hill
we'll battle hand to hand

You'll need but just one musket ball
the enemy is to close
There'll be no time to reload
or check for calvary's approach

Hold God in your heart today
and speak to him before you leave
Many of you brave brothers
will find peace in heavens reprieve

And for those who survive the battle
each one of you shall know
You've done it for our nation
so that our children stay free and grow

Poetic Perspectives

We do this today for our black and enslaved
To free families torn apart
ALL OF THE BLACK UNION FORCES....
NOW MUSTER!.....fight from the heart

Now as it was envisioned
I sit atop my steed and pray
Looking down upon that battlefield
where my brave black soldiers lay

I don't really understand the need
for slavery or the fight
Why real men can't see through this
end injustice and do what's right

Tonight I'll write my journal
tell the story of this place...
Black men who died with honor
to free an enslaved race

Jerrel E. Wolfe

Death March

I stand upon the battlefield
sabre clenched in trembling hand
Staring throughout the morning mist
and the barren blood soaked land

Another charge will come today
the boys will rally so
I savor all the memories
of the lives I've come to know

Should they not return this day
perhaps neither so shall I
I pray to God what we've done is just
and accepted in your eye

The calvary now ready
nervous horses snort their breath
Cannons are aligning
I see the face of death

I know nothing of my enemy
their loving wives and tiny tots
The sun begins to peak o'er the hill
my stomach's tied in knots

The General's now saddled
distant tree line becomes clear
The thundering sound of cannon
awakens my deafened ear

The sabre now is held high
waived in reflected morning sun
Each man making peace with his maker
The death march has begun

Jerrel E. Wolfe

Today's War

THREE SOLDIERS DIE AT CHECKPOINT
was the headline of the day
Another Iraqi bomb explodes
men simply blown away

It seems it is a daily strife
for the military of today
Not knowing where or when life will end
on any given day

There are sons and their are fathers
women with children too
What drives these valiant soldiers
to see a victory through

The bullets just might kill you
in this senseless morbid game
Saving people from the wrath
of the factions of Hussein

Did you go to bed and think last night
did you take the time to pray
For the soldiers that sacrifice their life
that have just been blown away

Poetic Perspectives

Survivors when they come home
do you call them out by name
Or are you just a greedy one
in a land of wealth and fame

Today you've read this picture
seen it from your heart
It's time to support our troops
and bless them at their start

And when they return to our shores
will you honor them – this way
Find a place in your heart
to pray for them each day

Think not only of those we have lost
but how many lives we've saved
Look at war from their perspective
then change will come your way

God has asked no more no less
of the soldiers of today
Than the price paid by his Son
whose life was swept away

Jerrel E. Wolfe

Owed Respect

The breeze was stiff the air was crisp
at Arlington this day
Former soldiers of past battles
had gathered here to pray

The sound of taps echoed
past the headstones where men rest
The heroes lost in battle
who did their very best

I see stars and stripes unfurling
half masted in the sky
Visions of drawn carriages
saluted passing by

I stand in puddled water
surrounding immersed shoes
Imagining the tear drops
and the lives we so did lose

I chose to walk this path today
we veterans travel a long long way....
Just to offer reverend respect for this
to commune and sit and pray

Poetic Perspectives

Oh what a mighty nation
we have build o'er centuries past
Not often taking time to praise the men
who have made it come to pass

Forefathers and their wisdom
soldiers brave and true
Gave us all they had to give
until their life was through

Jerrel E. Wolfe

Respected Sacrifice

The battlefield is quiet now
the mist hangs low to the ground
There is no more screams of pain
or rumbling cannons sound

There are no bloodied bodies
no shells or cannonade
Just silent memories
of supreme sacrifices made

Oh you didn't quit in battle
or the charges you have made
And for all your efforts
this memorial we have made

To honor you with salutes
and heads bowed low with pain
It was but for your sacrifice
the victories we have gained

Poetic Perspectives

An Honored Gift

The gates of Eternal Rest
were parted one winter's day
So I followed fresh tracks in the snow
to see what went this way

Before I could crest the hill
and look to the other side
A rifle blast pierced the peace
nested doves took to the sky

Another volley another blast
occurred before I could see
An honor guard of blue and white
erect in the snow covered scenery

And too the left beneath the oak
a flag draped coffin on a stand
One lone officer and a chaplin
and a single trumpeter for a band

The taps echoed into the clear blue sky
sun glinted off the snow
For who was this man being honored
what greatness did he bestow

Jerrel E. Wolfe

I walked up to the grave side
and took a place by the chaplin's side
Removed my hat to pay respect
for this patriotic pride

A soft voice said "God protect this man
as we send him off your way
He served his country with honor
and gave his life away."

"He volunteered for a mission
he new the risk quite clear
As a result of this man's actions
our president's still here."

"He had nobody in his life
no children or a wife
His bravery thwarted a terrorist
and thus he gave his life."

The colonel then handed me a flag
the reason I know not
He said this was a parting gift
from the country for which he fought

Today that flag sits on the mantle
I view and ponder it every day
Thanking God for the red white and blue
and the trek I took that day

Jerrel E. Wolfe

To your honor

There are battlefields and grave yards
throughout the USA
Biographies and memories
strewn along the way

The men who fought and died for us
we never can repay
For neath those stones lie the bones
of men just blown away

Why was there that big battle
just what was it all for
The pain the hurt that it all caused
we'll feel for ever more

When I look upon the fields
where battles have been played
I focus on the headstones
where the heroes have been laid
Then look up to the heavens to pay an accolade

It was they who made the sacrifice
so we could live life here
Freedom justice liberty
and life lived free from fear

At Rest

A life destroyed the essence gone
of a true devoted friend
Shot in the head and now he's dead
such a wonderful life to end

At thirteen he became my soulmate
we played most every day
Adopted from a family
forced to give him away

Accepted and loved
from the very start
There was never any question
of love given from the heart

In the short time that he spent with me
I could see thankful devotion in his eye
He couldn't ever speak a word
our time did fly right by

There'll be many nights I miss him
the love he shared for me
The tears I cry this solemn day
will be felt for eternity

Jerrel E. Wolfe

It's not for us to understand
when life will come to end
Perhaps he's in a better place
my faithful four-legged friend

Stryker was a loving lab
trained to help one see
He served his loving master
five years plus another three

When age forced his retirement
now replaced...he had to go
Abandoned in the sunset years
and the life he'd come to know

I was the special lady
who looked into his eye
Fell in love with his faithfulness
and could not let him die

I promised him a good home
love and labs to play
Made him my companion
as a tribute I did pay

Poetic Perspectives

He found a second childhood
in the short time he was here
Once I saw him bolt down the path
He thought he saw a deer

He never left my bedside
my feet he warmed at night
Stryker was the best of labs
he was educated right

And then while enjoying a reward
a special loving treat
He found himself choking...
a challenge too old to beat

This loving devoted labrador
was not meant to die this way
To suffer after all his work
was too high a price to pay

I tried to save my loving friend
and realized my worst fear
There was no hope for Stryker
I had to end it here

Jerrel E. Wolfe

With tear filled eyes I placed the gun
to the side of Stryker's head
Took one look into his eyes
in a moment he was dead

Now as I sit about
and view autumns setting light
I feel so awful sorry
but I know what's done is right

Stryker you will always walk with me
and be right by my side
When I walk on darkened nights
I know you'll be my guide

Candy

The burning embers crackled
in the fireplace late last night
As my faithful canine companion
sat fireside in sleepful delight

The paws would twitch and a muffled bark
could be heard as I stroked her coat
Perhaps we play together in her dreams
...Just a thought, I thought, I'd note

Perhaps she sees me standing
running and playing ball
Perhaps she sees me as I was
before I took that fall

She saved me on that Icy night
at the bottom of the stairs
As I laid there in the frigid cold
wondering if anyone really cares

Three miles she ran in the dark of night
in answer to my plea
Brought back three grown children
who helped to rescue me

Jerrel E. Wolfe

Today in this chair I sit
and reminisce this Christmas eve
Staring at four packages
beneath my Christmas tree

There's special gifts for Charles
Christopher and Sulli
And a big red one wrapped with all my love
for my faithful lab named Candy

Poetic Perspectives

Trick or Treat

Two hundred years had come and gone
where the house stood on that hill
The barren trees had lost their leaves
and the mood was eerie still

A full moon cast a shadow
of the witches peak that night
As the clouds moved past the aura
creating a very scary sight

Ghosts and ghouls there are none
that's what my teachers say
But for a bar of candy
should I walk up that pathway

My mom says I'm a big boy
for the age of four
She's sitting back in the car
...I have to knock upon that door

Where are the other kids tonight
it seems they've gone away
Perhaps I have enough tonight
I'll simply walk away

Jerrel E. Wolfe

"LITTLE MAN, come on up here"
a voice pierced throughout the night
Startled me as I turned around
I felt a little fright

Up there on that darkened porch
an old lady there did stand
Smiling down upon me
with a gift held in her hand

GRANDMA, why'd you do that
wait for me to go
Then yell down those long dark steps
as If I didn't know

I knew this was your house
I knew it all the time...
I was just checking in on my mom
I left her right behind

Poetic Perspectives

Ghosts ships of Nantucket

The fog on Nantucket seashore
is heavy this time of year
The throngs of summer visitors
have traveled far from here

With the autumn season
the leaves fall to the ground
Echoing in the distant mist
you'll hear the fog horn sound

The rhythmic beacon signs its light
piercing through this cloud
And I an aging mariner
vision ghosts ships off port bow

Silently they glide
through the misting light
Creaking wooden decks sound out
on this hallowed night

A pirate and a yeoman
scallywags with their beards
Hang from the masted riggings
that mortal men had feared

Jerrel E. Wolfe

All heading out from harboured port
entering into the night
To sail the rocky northern coast
casting shadows from lighthouse light

This is not a night to be outdoors
though the local pub does call
Heed the chills that rake your body
keep your back against the wall

Be cautious fellow mariners
walk cautiously I implore
Each halloween a sailor disappears
as the fog rolls to the shore

Poetic Perspectives

The Haunted Saxophone

In the wee hours of a darkened night
lit only by the Crescent Moon
You can hear the sound of the Haunted Sax
In most any hotel room

For in that shop on St Philip
where the Blues is often played
Not by the talents in the city
but by a soul that has been laid

Paulette has found a home in here
amongst many curious things
Spirits of a former Church
and those attached to many rings

A gifted ear may hear that tone
of a lady heavy burdened
Her anger and the Haunted Sax
Overshadows that on Burbon

So it's here she rests
untouched from the Quarters masses
Ensuring no man can ever blow the sound
of the saxist of the town of Natchez

Jerrel E. Wolfe

Easter Wish

To those who are slightly spiritual
who haven't completely committed to Christ
Know that on this special day
one man paid a price

Because of all his suffering
his willingness to bear our sins
Isn't it but a small request
to begin our lives again

So on this Easter Sunday
believe and know all this
The pathway that has unfolded to you
can eventually lead to bliss

A kingdom there awaits you
and a journey you must take
Let Easter be the first day
commit to God for Heaven sake

Poetic Perspectives

Heavens Valentine

Another Valentine's day has rolled around
and in my heart the friends I've found...
To cherish and have to reap
their kind and cheerful words to keep

For the deep love of years gone by
has been ripped and taken from this guy
Who up and gave all of himself
to be thrown away despite all his wealth

In the months that have since passed
many hours have been spent looking in that glass
Faith has brought the opportunity
to look through that glass and finally see...

That love and friends are all around
family ties are strongly bound
The world moves on as do I
reaching for stars in a celestial sky

Jerrel E. Wolfe

Thinking not of years gone by
but readying for my next great ride
Receiving a Valentine of love
placed in my heart by the Man above

With new direction and a path now chosen
life moves on from what once was frozen
An endless Valentine of love
continually delivered from the Lord's white glove

Poetic Perspectives

A Christmas Book

Another Christmas present
given out on Christmas day
Another piece of paper
to discard and throw away

And as I opened up the gift
a book appeared to me
A Billy Graham inscription
a book of which to read

Once getting past the cover
I found a book mark placed inside
Upon opening up this book
I found a message which could not hide

"Through adversity God reminds us
that he wants us to give Him control of our life"
I pondered this profound thought
and how it related to my wife

You see a year had come and gone
since torn from the family
She said she was not happy
with husband kids and bakery

Jerrel E. Wolfe

The job was to stressful
the kids to much a chore
A husband providing life's support
not as exciting as before

This Christmas there are now three of us
two dogs and a couple cats
A vacancy in the household
with the husband wearing all the hats

A peaceful merry Christmas
was found for us this year
Even though so many months
were filled with desperation and much fear

It came from His direction
and the path He put us on
Protected us beneath his wing
when I open up my arms

You see this valued quote I read
is so true and common sense
That God's the one to get you through
as you walk in His presence

Poetic Perspectives

This Christmas book just reminds me
of a path I chose to choose
...many months before
I avoided the Christmas blues

Jerrel E. Wolfe

Let Us Win

Just a hit just one more run
that is all we really need
Please dear God let us win this game
my ego needs to feed

I've done my best
and worked so hard
Please don't give up on this team
My parents are intently watching ...
it's the only game they've seen

(At bedtime)

The last time I spoke to you
I ask you for your help

You ignored my plea to rescue me
and save my team today
You left me down without a sound
I no longer wish to play

(That night In a dream)

Poetic Perspectives

Hello dear son who ask of me
such a small request
I heard your call to control that ball
and grant your happiness

Don't think that I ignored you
there was a lesson learned today
I looked down upon you
and decided things this way

I could make one team happy
I could make one team sad
There were 18 prayers said to me
others from coaches others from dads

I held in admiration
the trust you placed in me
I honor your commitment
and the fact that you're Godly

Your old enough to understand the problem
dealt me this day
Why I had to sit back
and enjoy the way you play

Jerrel E. Wolfe

You really didn't lose this game
you won it from the start
We all cheered in heaven
when you opened up your heart

Abandoned

It was but a simple delivery
to a rest home by the bay
A place to house the elderly
and folks just thrown away

And there upon that wrap around porch
...sitting in a chair
An aged woman with so much grace
and beautiful silver hair

I asked her if she knew a lady
named Clara Hatterly
She said "Why yes I do young man
she sits down there.... I'm one hundred three."

Each wrinkle on her smiling face
had a story to tell
And I a recent retiree
could see it all so well

The masted ships moved serenely by
as we peered out toward the bay
She asked me to sit down a spell
and pass the time of day

Jerrel E. Wolfe

Suddenly it came over me
a sense 'ner felt before
Those flowered daily deliveries
didn't mean much any more

She smiled and said quite warmly
" I appreciate your time
The Lord will call me home tonight
my children I can't find."

"They thought I was a burden
my needs they could not meet
They left me here ten years ago
and walked off down the street."

"Oh Johnny was a good boy
he played ball when he went to school
Patty was a hair dresser
...worked harder than a mule."

"You know they really are good kids
just so busy don't you know
They said they'd come to see me
...that was about three Christmas's ago."

Poetic Perspectives

...Twas then I reached out and grabbed her hand
and placed it in my palm
Told her I just saw her kids
they were at the park just singing songs

Her grand kids had new babies
all just as healthy as could be
Everyone was happy
just too busy...so they sent me

I placed that bouquet of flowers
there upon her lap
Told her that her family
placed all their love in that

With that came a precious smile
a grin from ear to ear
"I knew my children loved me
and that's what brought you here."

"I'm tired young man
I have to go I need a little rest
I'll be traveling on a journey tonight
and I need to look my best."

Jerrel E. Wolfe

"Could you call the nurse before you leave
as she placed a tender touch
Tell my children I'll see them soon
and I love them oh so much."

With that said, ...I left her
sitting in that space
Walked out toward the setting sun
as a tear streamed down my face

I didn't even get her name
but I fell in love that day
The day I delivered flowers
to the rest home by the bay

Chicago

The car sped round the corner
the gun went rat-a-tat
I pictured myself on a Chicago street
about seventy -five years back

I stood there with my sweetheart
with her fine haberdashery
Huddled up against the wall
in hopes gangster bullets were not meant for me

The windows in that corner shop
were shattered on the ground
Stepping from the lacquered Packard
two well dressed thugs did abound

They made their way past the rubble
and entered through the screen
Returning with a stately man
whom I had never seen

They placed him in the waiting car
and then just sped away
Leaving frightened pedestrians
to watch in sheer dismay

Jerrel E. Wolfe

A common sight on city streets
In an era when mobsters ruled
Store keepers learned to keep mouths shut
for lessons of oppressive violence had been schooled

We continued down the darkened street
and near a far streetlight
We heard the sound of Duke's big band
...Care to charleston tonight?

Past the guarded entrance
into the smoke filled hall
The flappers and the dappers
were having quite a ball

There was alcohol a plenty
and damsels ruled the night
Gentlemen with slicked hair
were visioned left and right

A ragtime tune scorched the air
as the patrons laughed with glee
Another round of bootleg...
rot gut whiskey for you and me

This time...the roaring twenties
is Americana of the past...
I WAKE...with etched memory
an era that couldn't last

Jerrel E. Wolfe

Selma

Not far from the diner
in a park near Pettus bridge
I speak of southern history
to my children and their kids

It's been a hundred years
since the president made his speech
By now you would think my children
could safely walk the streets

Not the case here in 'bama
when the sun sets on this town
We lock ourselves within our doors
there's no one to be found

Tomorrow we make history
we'll march across that span
We'll take our case to Montgomery
and do the best we can

We know they will try to stop us
beatings we will take
I pray that no more lives be lost
Now Martin holds our fate

Poetic Perspectives

The Mayor and the Governor
the President at the top
Still will not release the grip
this battle must be fought

So I'll take the challenge
maybe marching to my death
I will not raise a clenched fist
should I breathe the final breath

I know that God is with me
I don't question why it's so
The devil's got his grip on us
and marching I must go

Jerrel E. Wolfe

Origami

Take a piece of paper
fold the edges tweak a a knot
Flip it over start again
and see just what you've got

They call this art Origami
for what reason I don't know
It's just a folded paper
a bird a box a bow

From just a simple piece of parchment
an art form you will find
Just use your imagination
it doesn't matter if you're blind

There's something very soothing
to fold and give away
The treasures that you make up
when your heart folds gifts this way

At Christmas there are angels
with wings arched from their back
Easter bunnies and springtime flowers
and various knicks and knacks

Poetic Perspectives

You'll charm the eldest senior
and place smiles upon young faces
This art of Origami
will take you many places

So the next time you undertake a challenge
to see what you can do
Fold a simple piece of paper
It's Origami when your through

Jerrel E. Wolfe

In God We Trust

Did you ever pause to think one day
why we say In God We Trust
As you travel down lifes winding road
an answer is a must

The men who built the nation
where we live free from fear
Came up with this slogan
to draw people far and near

Imagine if you lived your life
in a distant foreign land
Where oppression ruled
little food and never a helping hand

You saw a piece of currency
a special color green
A special message on it
it couldn't helped be seen

"In God We Trust" sent a message
and an image it portrayed
Of better times a better place
seeds of hope are laid

Poetic Perspectives

You see this as a calling card
to all who need our love
To offer peace and harmony
this bill is blessed above

So when you think so selfishly
of what it might not mean to you
Think about the hope it brings
and the men who truly knew

Jerrel E. Wolfe

The Postal Carrier

Winter's air comes quickly
as autumns leaves fall from the trees
The crisp bite of the morning
says pull out the longer sleeves

Those days of tanning sunshine
are dwindling very fast
The warmth of a shallow sun
cast longer shadows and makes me ask...

What purpose do the seasons have
and why do they come this way
Autumn's harvest of covered fields
yields to snow covered piles of hay

With the freeze nature becomes quite still
the birds have left the sky
No morning sounds as I make my rounds
for this delivery guy

A crunch is heard beneath my feet
as I tread through hardpack snow
I yearn to see the spring again
my frosted cheeks now glow

Poetic Perspectives

A cup of coffee warms my heart
I'll seek to stay inside
Till the morning calls once again
and I cast my warmth aside

Jerrel E. Wolfe

I Found It In Miami

They called it South Miami
Pristine beaches filled with sand
The neon and art deco
and the sound of a summer's band

It was there I looked upon you
such a man to be seen
We strolled the starlit beach that night
viewing the reds blues and green

That kiss at the seaside
with the brine swirling through our toes
Connected deep inside me
and fought off all my woes

Was it love discovered on that beach
on a moonlit summers eve
When I released myself into your arms
opened all for you to see

My hands trembled upon your chest
as I reached beneath the silk
Bared the shoulders of a love embrace
my heart and soul did tilt

Poetic Perspectives

And as u placed upon me
your tender lips so fine
I knew right then I wanted you
till the end of time

Time has past and distance stands
between those thoughts and thee
I question on rainy nights
will you be there for me

I don't have all the answers
actually there's none that I can show
In nightly dreams I search the beaches
for the love I've come to know

Jerrel E. Wolfe

I Am The Seasons – You Are The Wind

I wallowed in late springtime
my life was just a mess
You moved me with the gentleness
of the breeze that you possess

With summer moving slowly
natures touch became quite real
Your sporadic clouds did pass me by
as my tender heart did heal

Like a whirlwind you possessed me
with lightening you did strike
Summer quickly passed right by
and now Autumn is in sight

This Autumn stands majestic
in early summer sunsets
You blow wrinkled leaves across my shadows
cool the soul and its regrets

Poetic Perspectives

The briskness of your morning touch
hearkens goose bumps on chilled nights
I inhale your wholesome goodness
viewing formation fowl in southern flight

The early morning exhale
shows Autumns misted kiss upon the glass
I hear the crackle of crushing leaves
neath my feet along running paths

You've moved me to this moment
the next step obviously is mine
With winter around the corner
One final wind gust I will find

Moving to the new year
a newness will begin
Natures forces and time together
Leaving history in your wind

Jerrel E. Wolfe

Taken

My baby's in your arms tonight
right where she needs to be
Rescued from a world of hate
lost morals and insanity

You know this was quite tough for me
to pass her on this way
I needed a little time to spend with her
before sending her on her way

Lord I know you know what's best
I have total faith in you I trust
I know you have a special place
for children loved so much

If you get a chance please tell her
her mother loves her so
Tell her all about me
so her love will grow

When we meet in heaven
and I've come home to rest
I'll thank you first for accepting her
without this earthly test

Father Time

Today I shared a memory
with my aging dad
A memory of childhood
and a life I never had

The years given children
should be used as intended so
For real life's filled with many stresses
strewn along the path of which we go

There are birthdays and holidays
picnics and ball games
Candies and travel
and loved ones of many names

There would always be a chore to do
and work was left undone done
Never was there any time
to recapture the love of youthful fun

I missed the bed time stories
the hugs along the way
Where's acceptance of a son
who needed nurtured every day

Jerrel E. Wolfe

You see...there were no gifts of love
given to this boy
Never a loving moment
nor a Christmas toy

The love all came from mother
it never came from dad
The bonding that I needed
lost forever it was sad

Today on the downhill side
a half century has passed
The heartless man I call my dad
is aging very fast

He's heard my childhood story
I think it touched him deep inside
This man that still walks the earth
with a son he can't confide

So let this be a lesson
to fathers far and near
Spend time with your children
keep an open ear

Spread your time and love out freely
for them to see it so
Let your children enjoy their youth
before they have to grow

Jerrel E. Wolfe

Recipe for Life

Take a loving mother and one loving Dad
mingle them together showing all the love they have
Bake it two seventy or somewhere there about
pull it from the oven you'll hear it start to pout

This is where your real task begins
where you'll be challenged the most
To add the right ingredients
to insure you're a perfect host

With smiles and love
continually stir in...
A dose of cheer and happiness
to keep structure there within

At three a smidge of honesty
and stir some honor at this stage
Like yeast it will continually rise
taste blossoming with coming age

There are varied bakers opinions
on the mix this tort shall see
Correct amount of education
varies for you and me

Poetic Perspectives

Instill some dedication
concentration and lots of nap
Grow this combination
for several years and now look back

It's now the final touches
needed in this recipe
Hygiene and some grooming
and Oh Yes !...Faith for God to see

Let stand this treat
covered with a warm smile
Check it often
not just once in a while

And when eighteen years
have come to pass
Unleash this your goodness
to the mass

You'll reap the rewards of
a job well done
A blue ribbon recipe
you will have won

Jerrel E. Wolfe

Thanks will come
from far and near
But none as sweet
as the child you reared

The Fishin Hole

I see my grandson's freckles
as he sits beneath the tree
Fishing pole in hand
staring intently as can be

I've fished this hole since '41
it's been real good to me
Fed my struggling family
with the fish the Lord provided me

For years now it's just been a pleasure
to come down to this old stream
Catch a few release a few
and just sit back and dream

Not too much has changed here
when I view it from where I stand
Sure the highways and the cities
have grown all across the land

You see it's still quite peaceful here
This is where I use to play
Now in my twilight years
I'll pass it off today

Jerrel E. Wolfe

Grandson why don't you sit right down here
next to your old granddad
I want to share a special gift
handed down from my granddad

From today on...this is your spot
a place to dip your pole
Respect this sanctuary
it's now your fishin hole

The Lord's seen fit to give me space
to ponder life's great tasks
When you have entered manhood
this is all I'm gonna ask

Each time you fish this fishin hole
check the man you have become
Make the needed changes
so your world won't be overrun

Live your life with honor
good deeds and be of cheer
Don't forget to check yourself
each and every year

Poetic Perspectives

If in time...a little left of here
you hear a big old splash
Pay no mind just smile and know
It's me...pullin out a big ole bass

Jerrel E. Wolfe

The Zoo Keeper

Each day of life's a blessing
my work's become part of me
Tending to God's creatures
and loving them you see

I can hardly wait to punch the clock
and walk upon their land
The excitement is continually building
as they kiss my outstretched hand

The monkeys scream with pleasure
as they swing around their cage
The bears stand up and raise their paws
as if actors on a stage

The otters take their morning dip
and wave their flippers up to me
The seals bark out a morning chant
as I look into their sea

A giraffe reaches down…I scratch his chin
and pat him on the nose
"Feel the love my tall tall friend
from your head down to your toes."

Poetic Perspectives

The lions and the tigers
purr with my loving touch
The world thinks they're so viscous
"I think not so very much. "

The llamas congregate around the fence
to greet me every day
Birds walk in my footsteps
in hopes something might fall their way

There's so much joy and pleasure
in the job that I hold here
I feel kind of like a Noah
time passes year to year

Not too much has changed here
in my thirty years in this place
God's creatures appreciate the care I give
and await my smiling face

You too will be accepted
when you enter through the gate
Bring the children have a picnic
enjoy the zoo....please don't wait

Jerrel E. Wolfe

Summoning of the White Horse

Throughout the distant sunlight
amidst the smoke and plunder
I saw a figure on the hill
standing there amongst the kill

Four legs of beauty
had done his duty on this dreadful day
I struggled to one knee to see
all drenched in blood in a crimson sea

A pristeen steed with head held low
as if inside that he would know
The sacrifice made here today
where on this field so many lay

And now as the light of day grows dim
I do attempt to summon him
With gentle tender motions made
he notices the shining sabre blade

All energy drained I fell again
and dreamed of pleasant times
With deep respect he made the trek
to be here by my side

The warmth of his breath summoned
me and gave me strength to rise
His kneeling stance gave me a chance
as I looked into his eyes

From where he came I know not
but he was there for me
Outside this carnaged battlefield
was where I ought to be

With gentle steps he carried me softly along the way
all energy spent together we went on this solemn day
With trust in him I settled in
with nothing more to say

This steed of white traveled through the night
as if guided by a power
In my heart I knew
that this could not be the final hour

Jerrel E. Wolfe

Then in the mist I saw the lights
of a distant sheltered sight...and thought...
An angels there with long dark hair
to help me through this night

I visioned her softness her tender loving touch
eyes deep as the sea
A person my steed found
in his attempt to rescue me

I awoke in her arms and cried with relief
thanking my stallion steed
Honoring the love of a woman sent from above
who was ultimately there for me

Poetic Perspectives

Soulmate

Should you ever lose a soulmate
a heart that you have won
You'll never have an earthly peace
your current life becomes undone

There are many loves that you might find
friends and lovers throughout time
Soulmates are far and in between
the glue that makes your life grow green

You may give your love in marriage
your honesty and trust
Many years will go by
before dust turns back to dust

In that time I challenge you
to find a heart that's true
One that will always be there
and hold you when you're through

To kiss you on your last day
and receive your final gift
The passing of your soul through a heart
that forever will reminisce

Jerrel E. Wolfe

Soulmates rarely walk the earth
they're usually found above
Waiting for each other
in the beauty of unearthly love

Summers Gone

The ceiling fans are quiet now
the summers heat is gone
Autumns crisp chilling bite
has shocked flowers on the lawn

The pools water has no ripples
the scene is quite serene
No joyous sounds of summer
or playful visions to be seen

Misting fog lifts from the river
the trees are not as bright
The sun seems to set much earlier
it lengthens out the night

Time past is but a memory
we must move on from here
A new season is upon us
it'll soon be end of year

Summer is now history
filed and stored away
Stories to be reminisced
on a blistery winters day

Jerrel E. Wolfe

A Place In Time

The city street was quiet with a fresh
blanket of new fallen snow
blanketing the pavement sidewalk park and trees
The aging lamp lighter steadily made his rounds
despite arthritic knees

He'd tip his hat to the carriage driver
as the sled moved down the street
The sound of dancing bells and
clopping hooves made by horse's feet

Shop keepers brushed the snow
from their walks that winter's day
Children threw their snowballs
in the park across the way

There were lovers on the church steps
carolers by the wall
I the casual observer
was in admiration of it all

A light glowed in the church tower
you could faintly hear the sound
A train approaching the station
where families gathered round

Poetic Perspectives

I pictured a reunion
of loved ones gone away
Stepping from the railcar
to unite on Christmas day

I reached over and placed my present
at the far side of this miniature Victorian scene
Then marveled at the ornateness
of this enchanting holiday theme

It was done in such great detail
I could travel to this place
Becoming more than the scenery
I was held in its embrace

Oh what a simpler lifetime
where true love and joy exists
Would it be too much to ask
to live this Christmas wish

Jerrel E. Wolfe

Each Day

In the shadows of a darkened room
I hear your whispers

In the cool breeze of an autumn day
I feel your touch

In the garden of this mansion
I grasp your flowered scent

In the heat of the sunlight
I sense your warmth upon my neck

In each drink that passes o'er my lips
I taste your tender kiss

And each moment that I live this life
your presence I do miss

Poetic Perspectives

Growing, Growing, ...Gone

Sometimes in life we are forced
to become more than who we are
To grow up rather quickly
with life's challenges testing the bar

The pressures mount quickly
tasks we cannot perceive
Somehow summons inner strength
from deep inside of me

From daily childhood pleasures
to adult routines I go
Picking up all the pieces
of a major crushing blow

I do feel love around me
God's placed his tender hand
Upon me and my father
who is my only man

There's caring and concern
hugs and a needed kiss
Just the right remedy
for times such as this

Jerrel E. Wolfe

The future is quite misty
one that I cannot see quite clear
Its laid out before me
its time is drawing near

And as I prepare to leave
a house that I called home
To venture down a highway
...a new life for to roam

My life certainly has turned the corner
the past two months or so
From realizing where I've come
but not to where I go

Parents can't protect me now
they know not the path I take
It will be me and the Lord above
a journey we both shall make

Poetic Perspectives

Chess Master/Chess Charmer

Beneath the solar street light
along Decatur way
Sits the iconic figure
known as the Man in the Red Beret

Twas just about a year ago
with Christmas drawing nigh
I sat at this mans table
with a winners gleam in my eye

I thought I had the secret
the opening that can't be beat
A powerful mid game
with a spectacular closing feat

Alas it was not to be
as the master had last say
Pay your $5 bucks
Come back another day

Well that was then and this is now
at thirteen I'm much wiser
If the Master has a weakness
the clock might be the answer

Jerrel E. Wolfe

10 minute game I said with a smile
as he greeted me at his table
"Jude this is my mother, Jennifer"
dressed quite sultry in that sable

Jude gave his standard greeting
and jumped up from his chair
She batted her eyes layed a smooch on his beak
Was the master now blushing or just
reflection of his hat to his cheek

E4 E5
with each move she now spoke
The clock was now running
It's serious no joke

She asked him a question
he replied with a smile
She inquired of his history
his response took a while

Coffee for you
he said with a smile
It is a little bit chilly
I'll be here a while

Poetic Perspectives

Jude sprang from his table
and crossing the street
I looked at the clock
still ticking...how neat

He's now down to four
and I still have nine
I'll slow play this charmer
mom's doing just fine

Oh Jude that's quite tasty
and your charm is outstanding
We should have dinner
and possibly dancing

The check I had planned
he slipped with a castle
Jude's in a fight
and I'll give him a hassle

Now less than a minute
I lead with a rook
He slanted his bishop
my knight he just took

Jerrel E. Wolfe

With queen now exposed
I grabbed it with glee
With just 10 seconds left
he trapped knighted me

He winked at my mom
said your son is done
And offered his hand
with a smile

"Don't be sad young lad
you're really not bad
Your mom's the best distraction
I've ever had"

Poetic Perspectives

Breeching Death

There she blow's yelled the bowsman
as he stood upon his perch
Peering out into the ocean
to view the reason for this search

Magnificant and elusive
this whale of the raging sea
Now became the prey of man
and a hunt that tortured me

I had 'ner set foot on a vessel
and ventured from a port
But sometimes as a journalist
we must take adventures of this sort

I felt a fear come over me
as the men prepared the gun
The crew had filled the chase ship
...the mission had begun

This blue whale breached the surface
the gun discharged its spear
Past the spewing brine
the harpoon hit its mark so dear

Jerrel E. Wolfe

The crew of the chase boat
held on for the ride of their life
Ultimately for the prey they sought
this whale would undergo the knife

And now as I sit here
dim light of day cast on horizon
The workers fill the casks of oil
numbered by the dozen

Each piece of meat is tucked away
upon this merciless ship
I just sit and wonder
what's the point in all of it

This story I brought home with me
this whale now lights our town
Each evening when the lamps are lit
I hear echos of his dreaded dying sound

Poetic Perspectives

Independence Day

This special day comes once a year
where children marvel with delight
When fireworks fill the summer sky
and all waits for the night

It's the culmination of a day
that stands the test of time
A day we found our freedom
in a country oh so fine

Though most of us have given no thought
about this holiday
Men who fought to make this place
have died and gone away

Their signatures are etched on parchment
their bodies rest today
They once walked this land with honor
character led the way

So today when you see our flag
unfurling in the sun
Remember those who came and went
the victories they have won

Jerrel E. Wolfe

Our fathers and our brothers
of centuries gone by
Planted seeds of freedom
under stars and stripes raised high

The cause was just and righteous
all countrymen could see
The future of this promised land
and their growing family tree

Even as this day grows late
and flashes fill the sky
We need to 'ner forget the fact
that men have fought and died

To give us such great freedom
and the independence that we know
To live in the greatest country on earth
where fireworks end the show

Poetic Perspectives

New Beginnings

The conductor yelled "All Aboard"
the train steamed clouds of white
Passengers grabbed a final kiss
as they boarded this autumn night

The crispness of the evening air
mixed with the smell of cast iron steel
Brought an air of excitement
for all passengers to feel

East coast to the West coast
in just seven days I'm told
Riding on this steel clad horse
where a new life will unfold

St Louis, Virginia City and then
the city by the bay
A chance to start a new life
as I sit back and pray

In my past I leave behind me
the Big Apple and all its sights
The trials and tribulations
of the violence and street fights

Jerrel E. Wolfe

My family has all passed away
and I must seek my fate
Ride the rails and seek the trails
to the home I hope to make

There's a lady in my future
a nest for us to share
I'll search my soul to find the path
that will take me there

There's always new beginnings
one just has to take the step
Find the courage to move forward
and not look back with regret

Poetic Perspectives

Twilight Years

The twilights now descending
on a life lived over time
I've worked through all the seasons
penning many thoughts to rhyme

Surviving this earthly battlefield
and passing many tests
I see my failing body
and I know it needs some rest

So many things I long to do
so many hearts to touch
The way I spend these final years
could mean so very much

It's not about the me I seek
nor even family
But what will be the legacy
for all the world to see

It won't be about the money
the children or the wife
Or about all the effort
surviving all the strife

Jerrel E. Wolfe

I am just a common citizen
my poetry has impressed
I've laid this out on paper
to attempt to pass the test

I tried to lay the groundwork
in the decades that have past
Most often did my very best
to ensure my name would last

Yet other times I failed the test
and left God's work undone
Often praying for forgiveness
knowing Lord still calls me son

So on my simple headstone
the legacy should read
This poet was a man of God
his soul has now been freed

www.ingramcontent.com/pod-product-compliance
Ingram Content Group UK Ltd.
Pitfield, Milton Keynes, MK11 3LW, UK
UKHW041953230426
12048UKWH00008B/311

9 781990 695742